name

Faith Friend's name

Faith Friend's phone number

Faith Friend's e-mail address

Faith Friends Emergency Card

name

Faith Friend's name

Faith Friend's phone number

Faith Friend's e-mail address

Faith Friends Emergency Card

name

Faith Friend's name

Faith Friend's phone number

Faith Friend's e-mail address

Faith Friends Emergency Card

name

Faith Friend's name

Faith Friend's phone number

Faith Friend's e-mail address

Faith Friends Emergency Card

name

Faith Friend's name

Faith Friend's phone number

Faith Friend's e-mail address

Faith Friends Emergency Card

name

Faith Friend's name

Faith Friend's phone number

Faith Friend's e-mail address

Faith Friends Emergency Card

name

Faith Friend's name

Faith Friend's phone number

Faith Friend's e-mail address

Faith Friends Emergency Card

name

Faith Friend's name

Faith Friend's phone number

Faith Friend's e-mail address

Faith Friends Emergency Card

name

Faith Friend's name

Faith Friend's phone number

Faith Friend's e-mail address

LiVE IT!

Building Skills for Christian Living

Making a World of Difference

Abingdon Press
Nashville

Live It!
Building Skills for Christian Living

Making a World of Difference

Copyright © 2005 by Abingdon Press
All rights reserved

Scripture quotations in this publication, unless otherwise noted, are from the New Revised Standard Version of the Bible, copyright © 1989 by the Division of Christian Education of the National Council of the Churches of Christ in the United States of America, and are used by permission. All rights reserved.

Scripture quotations marked (CEV) are from the Contemporary English Version, © 1991, 1992, 1995 by American Bible Society. Used by permission.

If you have questions or comments, call Curric-U-Phone, 800-251-8591, a toll-free service available Monday through Friday from 8:00 to 4:00 Central Time. Calls at other times are recorded for response the next working day. Or e-mail Curric-U-Phone at curricuphone@cokesbury.com any time.

Editor: Marcia J. Stoner
Production Editor: Melanie Munnell
Design: Randall Butler
Cover Design: Roy Wallace III
Cover Photo: Ron Benedict

ISBN 0-687-05341-2

05 06 07 08 09 10 11 12 13 14 — 10 9 8 7 6 5 4 3 2 1

Manufactured in the United States of America

CONTENTS

About the Writer:

Steve Harvester
lives with his wife and
teenage son in Norwell,
Massachusetts. He is a
minister in The United
Methodist Church.

He has written Sunday
school curriculum for
several years.

HOW TO USE THIS BOOK

The *Live It!* series of short-term studies begin with the life issues facing tweens and use the Bible to help tweens develop skills that will help them to live as disciples of Christ today and throughout their lives.

Live It! can be used with tweens in a variety of settings. It is designed to be used with fifth- and sixth-grade students, with optional use up to seventh grade.

Live It! Settings

• Sunday school
• Wednesday nights
• Short-term studies coinciding with other short-term church events

Parental Involvement

There is an article on page 62 for parents. Please reproduce this article and send it home to parents so that they will know what their tweens are learning.

Each book of the *Live It!* series has six sessions for tweens and an optional "Tweens and Parents Together" session where tweens and parents can come together and develop better communication skills. This joint session can be done as part of your regular session time and setting, or you can have this session at a time when it can be expanded and an event like a meal can be a part of the experience.

You might wish to do a parenting class that corresponds to the same time frame as your tween sessions for the parents of your tweens. The parenting class could meet jointly with your tween class for the seventh session.

Faith Friends

It is very important to begin developing faith mentors/models for your tweens. This is a model for the very beginnings of a mentoring relationship. See page 63 for specifics on how to set up a Faith Friends program. You will want to involve your Faith Friends in your service project.

Inserted into this book there are "Faith Friends Emergency Cards." These cards are for your tweens to have contact information for their Faith Friends and also for Faith Friends to have contact information for the tween they have agreed to mentor.

WE'RE IN IT TOGETHER

THE POINT

God created us all, God loves us all, we all belong to God, and we are called upon to respect all human beings as children of God.

THE SKILLS

Tweens will:
• recognize that all people are children of God.
• begin to accept that they will make their own contributions to the well-being of the world.

THE BIBLE

Genesis 1:27-31; Matthew 28:16-20; Acts 10:34-35

THE PLAN

PREPARE yourself

Tweens have heard many times before that we are all God's children. They have also heard that they have skills and talents to use to follow God's will. Today's session will attempt to help them put these two realities together.

If the world is truly interrelated, then even the small things we do affect other people. If we truly believe that we are all part of

PREPARE your session

Stuff to collect:
☐ NRSV Bibles
☐ nametags
☐ markers
☐ construction paper
☐ glue
☐ scissors
☐ old magazines
☐ paper punch
☐ yarn or string
☐ blanket or pillow
☐ pencils and pens
☐ masking tape or pushpins
☐ cellophane tape
☐ world map
☐ index cards
☐ **"Affirmation of Us" poster, p. 64**
☐ **Faith Friends Emergency Cards**
☐ **Faith Friends Program Information, p. 63**
☐ **Service Project Helps, p. 60**
☐ **Reproducible 1A, p. 11**
☐ **Reproducible 1B, p. 12**

For ☀ *cool options*:
☐ craft supplies

Stuff to do:
1. Make photocopies of Reproducibles 1A and 1B.

2. Ask each tween to bring information about his or her heritage (see "Show and Tell" activity).

God's creation and that God loves all of creation, then that must guide how we live in the world.

• **Genesis 1:27-31** tells us that "God created humankind in his image,…male and female he created them." The Bible does not say that God created white people or black people, or Christians or Jews or Muslims, or rich people or poor people. It says God created humankind—and that means all of us. To respect God we must respect all of God's creation.

To be made in the image of God does not mean that we look like God, but rather who we are as a whole—our being, our soul, our ability to act for God in the world.

• In **Matthew 28:16-20** the disciples were commissioned by Jesus to "make disciples of all nations," again letting us know that God's salvation is open to people of all races and all nationalities.

• In **Acts 10:34-35** Peter says, "I truly understand that God shows no partiality, but in every nation anyone who fears him and does what is right is acceptable to him."

Help your tweens understand that there are all kinds of people out there, a lot of bad mixed in with the good. But whether they are bad or good does not have anything to do with their nationality or race, but whether they choose to live righteously as God would have them do. Also help them understand that God reaches out to all people, including sinners, as long as they live, and as long as there is even a small hope that they will accept God and learn to live righteously.

GATHER

Welcome and Tag Them Time: 5 minutes

If your tweens to do not know each other, have them write their names on nametags (or on nametags they make themselves with construction paper, markers, scissors, old magazine photos, glue, paper punch, and yarn). Invite them to create a nametag that "makes a statement" about who they are.

Game Time: 5-7 minutes

Mark two lines at opposite ends of your classroom space. Tell one of your tweens that it is his or her task to go from one line to the other without touching the floor.

Stuff–Welcome and Tag Them:

❏ nametags (or construction paper, scissors, old magazines, glue, paper punch, yarn

❏ markers

Stuff–Game:

❏ blanket or pillow

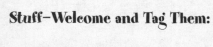 ❏ *cool options:* craft supplies

Live It! Making a World of Difference

Teamwork, of course, is the answer, so challenge the "rugged individual" in your group to accomplish the task. If the tweens figure out quickly that all they need to do is carry their fellow classmate across the room, add another condition to the challenge: tell them to get their classmate across the room without touching the floor, or anyone touching him or her. The tweens will need to put their friend on a blanket or a pillow and pull the blanket across the room.

INTERACT

Read and Talk About Scripture Time: 10-15 minutes

Seat your tweens in a circle. **Say: That was a tough challenge you took on together! Could the strongest kid in the class have done that alone? How about the fastest? How about the tallest? Who was needed to get the job done?** *(everyone)* By now the answer will be obvious to your tweens.

Ask one or more tweens to read Genesis 1:27-31. **Ask: Of all God's creations, which are most like God?** *(only human beings are created in God's image)*

Lead a short discussion on what it means to be made in the image of God. **Ask: What does this Bible passage tell you about what it means to be made in the image of God?** *(Of course, the biblical image tells them everyone is made in the image of God.)* You may wish to explain that that doesn't mean that we look like God, but rather that we are like God in that we have the capability to be "god-like" when we act righteously and follow God's ways.

Ask: Which country does God think is the greatest? Why do you think that? They are used to hearing people call the United States the greatest nation in the world. That may not be how God sees it.

Now, ask a volunteer to read Matthew 28:19. **Ask: According to this passage, what country does God think is number one? Do you think this surprised the disciples?**

Say: Just as we think the USA is number one, the disciples thought that Israel was "number one" with God. They could have known—because Jesus went to Samaria, and to the Romans—that God loves all people everywhere. But they still might have been surprised to learn they were supposed to love all people, everywhere, as well!

Cool Option: Give tweens a pile of craft supplies and tell them that they have to make a class craft. Give no other instructions. Watch the process and then let them talk about how they felt. Who was included? Who was not? How did they make decisions?

Stuff–Read and Talk About Scripture:

❑ NRSV Bibles

Making Connections Time: 5-10 minutes

Give tweens photocopies of "Making Connections" (**Reproducible 1A, p. 11**). Divide tweens into pairs or small groups. Have the groups work together to match the contributions made to the world with the correct country or part of the world it came from.

Bring the pairs/groups back together and quickly go over the list. Ask them what they see when they look at their completed papers (lines will overlap). Remind them that things are even more interconnected than they look on this paper.

Inventions and contributions don't just fall out of the sky; they are built on things learned before. For example, Edison's light bulb was not the first, but he was the first to be able to make light in a sustainable way. Leonardo da Vinci wasn't the first person to ever paint, but he built on all of the knowledge of light and color that came before. Pope John Paul II wasn't the first man to truly live a religious life devoted to God; first John Paul knew God, Jesus Christ, and the Holy Spirit, and was nurtured in the faith by others.

Answers:

Central America (Mayans)—rubber
China—fireworks, paper money
Cuba—salsa music
Egypt—sandals
France—Braille
Germany—Beethoven, contact lenses
Ghana (Ghana, Africa)—kente cloth
Great Britain—blood transfusions, Romeo and Juliet (the play)
India—curry, Mahatma Gandhi, sitar music
Iran—Persian carpets, spinach
Italy—batteries, Leonardo da Vinci
Japan—bullet trains, cultured pearls, flat screen TV
Poland—Pope John Paul II
Russia—nesting dolls
South Africa—Archbishop Desmond Tutu, heart transplants
South America—medicines from the rain forest
United States of America—electric lights, jazz music, polio vaccine

Live It! Making a World of Difference

I Can   Time: 10-15 minutes

Give tweens a photocopy of "I Can..." (Reproducible 1B, p. 12).
Tell them they have four minutes to select from the list five things
they can do to make this a better world. They are to work
individually. They can circle or underline each item that they are
willing to do. (Do not have them fill in the bottom lines yet.)

Call time at the end of four minutes. Then tell them you are going
to read each thing on the list. Tell them to stand up when you read
the items that they have marked and to sit down if it is not one
they have chosen. They can stand up no more than five times.

Quickly go through the list. This gives them an active way to
discuss things tweens can do to make the world a better place.

DEPART   Time: 5-7 minutes

Post the "Affirmation of Us" poster in a prominent place.

**Say: It really is a small world. All of us are created in the
image of God; all of us live in nations loved by God. Each of
us can help to make this world better. Right now, on your "I
Can..." sheet** (Reproducible 1B, p. 12) **write three things that
you will commit to doing this week on the three lines at the
bottom of the page. You can choose from the list or write
something of your own.**

Give them about three minutes to complete their lists.

**Say: Each of us helps to make this world different and
exciting in countless ways. Let's give God thanks for some of
the things that make it such a wonderful and exciting place
for us.**

Together read aloud the "Affirmation of Us."

Close with the Lord's Prayer.

Stuff—I Can:

❏ **Reproducible 1B,
p. 12**

❏ pens or pencils

Stuff—Depart:

❏ **"Affirmation of Us"
poster, p. 64**

❏ **Reproducible 1B,
p. 12**

❏ masking tape or
pushpins

❏ pens or pencils

PLAN PLUS

Making Connections Map Time: 15-20 minutes

After completing the "Making Connections" activity (**Reproducible 1A, p. 11**), tape a world map to the wall. Give each tween one or more index cards and assign them a country or region from "Making Connections." Ask each tween to write the name of his or her assigned country or region in the center of an index card. Then have them write the item (or items) listed on Reproducible 1A that were contributed by their assigned country/region. Have them tape a piece of string or long piece of yarn to their index card, tape the card to the wall, and run the string or long piece of yarn to where their country/region is located on the map. Have them tape the other end of the string or yarn at the corresponding location on the map.

Show and Tell Time: 20-30 minutes

If you have longer sessions (such as evenings), before the first session ask each tween to put together a "Show and Tell" based on her or his family heritage. If a tween isn't familiar with his or her heritage, and if he or she isn't able to get help from others in the family, then allow the tween to put together a show and tell on any culture that is intriguing. Information they bring for "Show and Tell" might include: music, art, architecture, stories of great leaders, family photos, traditional clothing, and so forth.

Service Project Time: 20-30 minutes

Making a World of Difference really needs a service project to go along with the sessions to touch the hearts and lives of your tweens. Glance quickly over each lesson to see where you might want to head with your mission/service project.

Read page 60 for suggestions on how to start up and carry out a service project for your class.

You will need to keep some time each week for checking on what's happening with your service project.

Faith Friends

If you are going to have a Faith Friends program, remove and separate the Faith Friends Emergency Cards. Refer to p. 63 for more information on the Faith Friends program.

MAKING CONNECTIONS

Draw lines to match the countries and/or regions of the world with some of the great people and/or things they have given us. (Countries and/or regions may have contributed more than one person or thing on the list.)

batteries	CENTRAL AMERICA (Mayans)	jazz music
Beethoven	CHINA	kente cloth
blood transfusions	CUBA	medicines from the rain forest
Braille	EGYPT	nesting dolls
bullet trains	FRANCE	paper money
contact lenses	GERMANY	Persian carpets
cultured pearls	GHANA	polio vaccine
curry	GREAT BRITAIN	Pope John Paul II
Leonardo da Vinci	INDIA	*Romeo and Juliet*
electric lights	IRAN	rubber
fireworks	ITALY	salsa music
flat screen TV	JAPAN	sandals
Mahatma Gandhi	POLAND	sitar music
heart transplants	RUSSIA	spinach
	SOUTH AFRICA	Archbishop Desmond Tutu
	SOUTH AMERICA	
	UNITED STATES OF AMERICA	

Reproducible 1B

I CAN...

Here are just a few things that can be done to make the world a better place.

List on the lines below three things you can do this week. You can choose from the list or do your own thing—as long as it makes the world a better place.

▲ treat others with respect.

▲ make music.

▲ make someone laugh.

▲ learn something new. (It might lead to something greater.)

▲ help clean up a disaster area.

▲ learn how to do something better.

▲ be kind when I don't feel like it.

▲ make a new friend.

▲ read a book about something I don't know anything about. (I might discover something new and important.)

▲ invite a friend to Sunday School.

▲ pray for someone who needs help.

▲ pray to be a better person each day.

▲ learn everything I possibly can about as many things as I can.

▲ make art that will bring joy to another person.

▲ write a letter.

I can _____

I can _____

I can _____

THE POINT

Now is the time to begin building a lifetime habit of sharing our time and talent with others. The Gospel principle of *agape* (selfless love) is the foundation for this way of life.

THE SKILLS

Tweens will:
• connect volunteering to Christian faith.
• understand that each Christian call is for an individual commitment.
• discover one way they can individually and/or collectively "feed God's sheep."

THE BIBLE

Isaiah 6:1-8; John 21:15-17; various biblical calls

THE PLAN

PREPARE yourself

Volunteering is something tweens love to do, though they often can't do so on their own because transportation and child labor laws can both be deterrents.

However, to provide meaningful learning in the area of the world and our relationship with it, service projects need to be a high priority. They will help tweens put faith into practice, and they have emotional content for tweens that will lead to lifelong learning.

PREPARE your session

Stuff to collect:
- ❏ NRSV Bibles
- ❏ any items necessary for tasks for the tweens to complete as soon as they enter the classroom
- ❏ scissors
- ❏ pens or pencils
- ❏ "Affirmation of Us" poster, p. 64
- ❏ Service Project Helps, p. 60
- ❏ Reproducible 2A, p. 19
- ❏ Reproducible 2B, p. 20
- ❏ Reproducible 2C, p. 59

Stuff to do:

1. Make photocopies of Reproducibles 2A, 2B, and 2C.

2. Cut apart the cards on Reproducible 2C.

3. Set up tasks for the tweens to complete as soon as they enter the classroom.

If you did not start last week, start now and help your tweens plan and carry out a service project. Also help your tweens look at (and perhaps begin) their own individual ways of volunteering. Let your tweens practice "feeding God's sheep."

Isaiah 6:1-8 is a passage about how Isaiah was called by God to be a prophet and Isaiah answered, "Here am I; send me!" There are many other Bible stories of calls and answers. And even today the call to do God's will for our lives is being heard and answered positively by many people (while others ignore the call or answer "No"). How we answer our call is crucial to our own personal salvation and to God's world.

John 21:15-17 is the last meeting between Jesus and Peter. In it Peter is asked three times, "Do you love me?" When Peter answers "Yes," Jesus tells him, "Feed my sheep." Here Jesus is telling Peter to carry on the mission of the church both spiritually and physically. Jesus well understood that it is difficult to minister to a person's soul if the person is hungry or so tired he or she can't focus. So feeding the sheep means taking care of all of the needs of God's people. Remember, the whole world is God's people.

GATHER

Who Will Volunteer? Time: 5-8 minutes

Have several things that need to be done ready so that you can ask tweens to volunteer to do them as they enter the room— enough so that everyone who comes early can "volunteer" to do something.

For example, nametags can be made (and/or passed out as people arrive); John 21:15-17 can be practiced for reading later; chairs can be arranged; reproducibles can be separated and put into two separate piles for later; some things can be cleaned up in the room, someone can greet newcomers; and so forth.

As tweens come in, let them know some of the things that need to be done and encourage them to "volunteer" for one of the tasks. Get them started on their assignment immediately.

When everyone has gathered, thank the volunteers for their help. (You will talk about these efforts a little more later.)

Stuff—Who Will Volunteer?:

❑ any items necessary for tasks for the tweens to complete as soon as they enter the classroom

Live It! Making a World of Difference

INTERACT

Called by God Time: 20-25 minutes

Before class make a photocopy of the "Called by God" Cards **(Reproducible 2A, p. 19)**. Cut the cards apart but keep each set divided into the correct categories. The four categories are: *Scripture Reference*, *Who Was Called*, *How Called*, and *Called to Do What*.

Say: A volunteer steps forward, often feeling a call to do so. In the Bible, people are called forward by God for specific tasks. Let's discover how some were called and what they did. Choose one of the following options to discover what the Bible tells us about calling.

Option One: If you have a small class, lay out the cards faceup on a table. Place the cards in the four rows depending on their categories, only mix up the order. Let the tweens figure out how to work together to get the cards into the correct order across with the four categories correct.

Teacher Tip: You might have to give them tips on how to divide up the work: some can use the Bibles, some can read off what is on the cards, while somebody else can move them around.

Option Two: Make a set of cards for each group of four or five tweens. Mix up all the cards of all four categories. On a board or large sheet of paper, write the four categories so that they can see them easily. Have the groups race to see which team can put all of their cards in the correct order first. (Again they will need to use their Bibles, and teamwork will make them faster.)

After they have finished the activity, discuss the following questions:
1. There were three people called to do things while they were very young. Who were they? *(Jeremiah, who was called before he was born; Samuel; and Timothy.)*
2. What are some of the differences in the ways they were called? *(Some were dramatic—a burning bush—and others like Timothy were raised in the faith and gradually became aware of their calling.)*
3. What do these calls have in common? How are they different? *(All of these people had their own plans for the future. None of them felt worthy of God's call. In each case, God made them worthy.)*
4. Where in your life do you hear God asking, "Whom shall I send?" How worthy are you?

Stuff–Called by God:

❑ NRSV Bibles

❑ scissors

❑ **Reproducible 2A, p. 19**

Teacher Tip: If time is short, you might reduce the number of calls that you have them work with or have different groups work with different calls, taping them under the categories on a large sheet of paper you have posted.

Stuff—Who's Doing What?:

❑ pens or pencils

❑ **Reproducible 2B, p. 20**

Teacher Tip: To avoid the forming of cliques, keep putting your tweens into new groups and/or pairs. This shuffling helps them learn to work with and develop relationships with all of their peers in the group.

Teacher Tip: The "Whom Shall I Send" activity is about individual volunteering, but you can also check Reproducible 2C for opportunities for a class service project.

Stuff—Whom Shall I Send?:

❑ **Reproducible 2C, p. 59**

Who's Doing What? Time: 5-8 minutes

Divide your tweens into new small groups or pairs. Give each group or pair a photocopy of "What Do They Do?" **(Reproducible 2B, p. 20)**. Ask them to write on the line beside each organization one or two things that each group does to take care of God's people. Then ask them to write down three things they could volunteer to do, either for these or other organizations.

Set a time limit. Read out each organization's name. Let them tell you what they put down. If there are groups whose mission they don't know, help them by telling them one thing the organization does.

Answers:

Room in the Inn: *Provides shelter for the homeless.*
Red Cross: *Collects blood for operations. Helps with disaster relief.*
The Salvation Army: *Among other things, helps feed and shelter the poor, and collects gifts for poor children at Christmas.*
Habitat for Humanity International: *Helps the poor build houses they can purchase interest-free.*
Heifer International: *Helps provide animals for the poor to start that their own herds so that they can become self-sufficient.*
Amnesty International: *Works to help free those put in jail for political reasons and to help prevent abuse of prisoners.*
UNICEF: *Raises money to help provide children around the world with food and immunizations against disease.*
Bread for the World: *Helps raise money to get food to the poor around the world. Works for legislation that will help fight hunger.*
My church as a denomination *(talk with your pastor before class).*
My local church *(talk with your pastor before class).*

Whom Shall I Send? Time: 5-8 minutes

Remind your tweens of the different calls that they have talked about during the lesson. Tell them that at different times in their lives they will probably be called by God to do different things. It is never too soon or too late to answer God's call.

Together talk about their experience when they first entered the room. Did they like volunteering? Why or why not? What would they rather have done? Did they feel like what they were doing really helped? Remind them that today they were "called" by their teacher to volunteer, but that the call to do God's work is real and might come in many different forms.

Give each tween a copy of "Whom Shall I Send?" (**Reproducible 2C, p. 59**).

Say: Sometimes it's difficult to know how to answer a call. We feel strongly that we are to do good and to help others, but we often don't know how. This short list of some types of possibilities are to help you start thinking of different ways you can answer God's call.

DEPART Time: 5 minutes

Say: When Jesus told Peter how he was to lead the church, his instructions were very simple. Let's read them now. Ask a tween to read John 21:15-17. (You may have asked someone to volunteer for this task as part of the "Who Will Volunteer?" activity earlier in the session.)

Say: Peter was an ordinary person like you and me. God made him worthy to perform a great task. The task was to take care of God's people, spiritually and physically. Every task that comes from God is a great task. There is a great task set before each one of you. God has sent the Holy Spirit. God has washed you clean with the water of baptism. You are strong. You are ready. Let's give God thanks for giving us a task to accomplish.

Pray your own prayer or use this one. **Pray: Dear God, who would lead us where you need us to go, we give thanks for your greatness and for your willingness to use us to do your work in the world. We are willing to accept the challenge. We each say to you: Here am I; send me. Amen.**

Close by reading together the "Affirmation of Us."

Stuff–Depart:

❏ NRSV Bibles

❏ "Affirmation of Us," p. 64

Stuff–"I Volunteer" Game:

❏ none

"I Volunteer" Game Time: 5 to 10 minutes

Have tweens sit in a circle and have them do a variation of the "alphabet game." Each person is to go in order and tell how he or she would volunteer by using the next letter in the alphabet. For example, the first person says: "I would volunteer to *Aid* the elderly." The second person would say: "I would volunteer to *Bring* refreshments." Continue with the next person using the letter *C*, and so forth. You may choose to stop after every person has had one turn, you may continue until you reach the letter *Z*, or you can continue until only one player is left. (In this version, if a person duplicates anyone else's answer, he or she is out of the game.)

Cool Option: In the original alphabet game, the second person repeats what the first person has said and then adds to it. The third person repeats what the first person has said, then what the second person has said, and then finally adds to it using the letter *C*.

Although this is time-consuming, if you have additional time, play the game this way for extra laughs and an emphasis on the varied opportunities.

Stuff–Service Project:

❏ **Service Project Helps, p. 60**

Service Project

Follow up on the service project your class chose last week. Take whatever step is necessary this week and make sure that everyone has an assignment.

Read page 60 for suggestions on how to start up and carry out a service project for your class.

You will need to keep some time each week for checking on what's happening with your service project.

Reproducible 2A

CALLED BY GOD CARDS

Scripture Reference	Who Was Called?	How Called?	Called to Do What?
Isaiah 6:1-8	Isaiah	a vision of God	to be a prophet
Jeremiah 1:5-6	Jeremiah	before he was born	to be a prophet
1 Samuel 3:1-18	Samuel	while sleeping	to be a judge
Exodus 3:1-4:17	Moses	burning bush	to free God's people from slavery in Egypt
Matthew 4:18-22	Simon, Andrew, James and John	while at work	to follow Jesus and learn
Matthew 28:16-20	the eleven remaining disciples	gathered on a mountain	to take the Gospel to all nations, baptizing and teaching people
Acts 2:36-47	the first converts to Christianity (about 3,000 of them)	Peter's Pentecost sermon	to learning, fellowship, breaking of bread, and prayers (living a God-filled life)
Acts 8:26-39	Ethiopian court official	Philip explaining the Scriptures	rejoice in the Lord
Acts 9:36	Tabitha (Dorcas)	unknown	to devote herself to good works and acts of charity.
2 Timothy1:1-5 and Acts 16:1-5	Timothy	raised in the faith by his mother and grandmother; asked by Paul to go with him	to help Paul strengthen churches in the faith.

WHAT DO THEY DO?

**Here are just a few places that need volunteers to do different things.
Do you know what each one does?**

Room in the Inn _____

Red Cross _____

The Salvation Army _____

Habitat for Humanity International _____

Heifer International _____

Amnesty International_____

UNICEF_____

Bread for the World _____

My church as a denomination_____

My local church _____

Three things I could volunteer to do:

MERCY: THE LOVE YOU CANNOT EARN

THE POINT

People make mistakes all the time. Jesus teaches us that to be in a right relationship with God we must learn how to show mercy, as our Father shows mercy to us.

THE SKILLS

Tweens will:
• begin to distinguish justice from mercy.
• start developing the ability to temper justice with mercy.

THE BIBLE

Matthew 18:21-35; Ephesians 4:31–5:2a (CEV)

THE PLAN

PREPARE yourself

Justice is what we cry out for, but perhaps we might be a little more reluctant to do so if we had justice applied proportionally to us. Have you ever yelled at someone in anger disproportionate to the offense? Have you cut someone off in traffic just because you wanted to be in the other lane? Have you ever told a lie to protect yourself?

Tweens are into the black and white of justice. They want justice meted out to the other guy, but beg for mercy when they have

PREPARE your session

Stuff to collect:

- ☐ NRSV Bibles
- ☐ two large sheets of paper or chalkboard and chalk
- ☐ scissors
- ☐ glue or tape
- ☐ pens or pencils
- ☐ markers
- ☐ ball (beach ball)
- ☐ plain sheets of paper
- ☐ **"Affirmation of Us" poster, p. 64**
- ☐ **Reproducible 3A, p. 27**
- ☐ **Reproducible 3B, p. 28**

For ☼ *cool options:*
- ☐ props and Bible-times costumes

Stuff to do:
1. Make photocopies of Reproducibles 3A and 3B.

For ☼ *cool options:*
2. Make arrangements for your class to go to an adult class to present "The Unforgiving Servant" drama

Mercy: The Love You Cannot Earn

strayed from the path—not so different from the way adults think, only more pronounced, and more often verbalized.

"That's not fair!" is the cry of the tween. As we look at life we realize that justice often needs to be tempered with mercy, that every offense does not have to be dealt with harshly. Forgiveness often does more than exacting justice.

Mercy, however, by its very definition, is forgiveness that is not earned. Mercy is forgiveness that is freely given with an open and loving heart. Every day, in many ways, we are shown mercy by God. To truly live in a right relationship with God, we too must learn to be merciful.

Many of Jesus' parables were about mercy: the prodigal son, the good Samaritan, and of course, the unforgiving servant. **Matthew 18:21-35,** the story of the unforgiving servant, will be used to help tweens understand that as God extends mercy to us, we are called upon to extend mercy to others.

Ephesians 4:31-5:2a (CEV) is the Bible verse for today. While NRSV is the Bible version used as the basis of these sessions, today's verse is best understood by tweens in the language of the CEV: "Stop being bitter and angry and mad at others. Don't yell at one another or curse each other or ever be rude. Instead, be kind and merciful, and forgive others, just as God forgave you because of Christ. Do as God does. After all, you are his dear children. Let love be your guide" (Ephesians 4:31–5:2a, CEV).

This verse is a summary of what today's lesson is about.

GATHER

Justice or Mercy Time: 5-7 minutes

Post two large sheets of paper on the wall (or divide a chalkboard in two with a chalk line). Label one sheet "Justice," and the other one "Mercy" (or if using chalkboard label each side of the board).

As tweens arrive ask them to write words that mean the same as justice or their own definition of justice under the word *justice* on the paper or board. Have them do the same with the word *mercy*.

Stuff–Justice or Mercy:

☐ two large sheets of paper and markers

OR

☐ chalkboard and chalk

Live It! Making a World of Difference

INTERACT

Defining Justice and Mercy Time: 2-3 minutes

Bring tweens together and look at some of the things they wrote about justice and mercy.

Say: **Justice is getting what you deserve. If you get every question right on a test at school, what do you deserve?** (allow time for responses) **If you didn't study and you cheated on the test, what would you deserve?** (allow time for responses) **At the very least you would fail the test. Some schools would suspend you for a time. That would be justice. When you cheat on a test, it is lying about what you know. It is a form of stealing, because you are stealing someone else's work and stealing a grade you didn't earn.**

Say: **What if it was the first time that you had ever cheated on a test, so the teacher decided that this one time you would be given a second chance and be given a make-up test? What would that be?** (allow time for responses) **Giving you the second chance without it going on your record would be called** *mercy.* **You didn't earn it, you have no right to it, it is freely given by someone who truly wants you to do better. That's what today's story is about. It is about mercy.**

Dramatize "The Unforgiving Servant"
Time: 20-25 minutes

Pass out copies of "The Unforgiving Servant" (**Reproducible 3A, p. 27**). Have tweens volunteer to play the characters in this dramatized version of Jesus' parable.

There is a lot of action in this story. Have the tweens actually act out the story, not just read it. When finished with the dramatization, **Ask: What do you think of each of the characters? What do you think Jesus was trying to tell you with this parable?**

Have them open their Bibles to Matthew 18:23. Ask one of the tweens to read the verse aloud. Tell them that this verse tells them that the story they just dramatized is about the kingdom of God.

Ask: Who would be the king in the story? *(God)* **Why do you think the king (God) was so angry with the first servant?** *(The first servant had been given mercy, yet he showed no mercy to the second servant.)*

Mercy: The Love You Cannot Earn

Stuff—Defining Justice and Mercy:

☐ lists made in "Justice or Mercy?" activity

Cool Option: Add costumes and props. Practice to present this drama to an adult class.

Stuff—Dramatize "The Unforgiving Servant":

☐ NRSV Bibles

☐ **Reproducible 3A, p. 27**

☐ *cool options:* props and costumes

Teacher Tip: Encourage them to over-dramatize, to ham it up. Tweens are more likely to internalize the message if they relate to it emotionally, and tweens relate strongly to overdone humor.

☐ scissors

☐ **Reproducible 3B, p. 28**

Teacher Tip: To shorten activity time, read the Scripture aloud before tweens try either option.

Answer: "Stop being bitter and angry and mad at others. Don't yell at one another or curse each other or ever be rude. Instead, be kind and merciful, and forgive others, just as God forgave you because of Christ. Do as God does. After all, you are his dear children. Let love be your guide."
(Ephesians 4:31–5:2a, CEV)

Ask a second volunteer to read Matthew 18:35 aloud.

In closing, **Say: Jesus is telling us in this parable that if we want mercy for our sins, then we need to learn to have a forgiving heart and treat others with mercy. It is not God's desire to treat us harshly, but rather that we should treat each other with mercy and love. However, we cannot expect God to treat us with mercy if we are unwilling to treat others mercifully. We have new chances to make this choice everyday.**

Scripture Scramble Time: 10 minutes

Help tweens actively discover today's Bible verse. Photocopy and cut apart the Scripture Phrase Cards (**Reproducible 3B, p. 28**). There are five sentences in this passage of Scripture. Depending upon time and number of participants, choose one of the following ways to have them put together the verses.

Option One: For a small class, mix up the Scripture Phrase Cards and place them face down in a pile on the table. One at a time the tweens will take turns drawing a card and trying to put it in its correct place. (Remember that they have no idea what the verses are yet, so they will make lots of mistakes; that's part of the fun, and the learning). After the second tween draws and places a card, the next tween must choose to either draw a new card or rearrange the cards already on the table. Play will continue like this until all cards are drawn.

At this point, they probably will still not have the verses correct, so read the verses to them (see answer in margin). Then let them quickly work together to put the verses in order.

Option Two: For a large class, pass out one or more of the cards to each tween. (Be careful if you give more than two cards; they must be in the same sentence.) Tell the tweens that there are five sentences in today's passage of Scripture and that they have one minute to find the people who they think have cards that are in their sentence.

Have them start, and then stop them after one minute. Have those who are in groups put themselves in what they think is the correct order of their sentence. There will be many mistakes and much laughter.

Give them one more minute and have them try again. After they have reported the second time, read the verses and then have them try to find those who have the cards they need.

Live It! Making a World of Difference

If they still don't have the correct order, read slowly and help them line up in their proper groups. Then have each tween read his or her phrase(s) aloud, starting with the first word of the first verse.

Mercy Ball   Time: 5-10 minutes

Have tweens help you move everything out of the way. Then have them form a large circle with everyone standing as far apart as is physically possible. Tell them that you will toss a ball (a beach ball works well) to someone. That person must say one way he or she can show mercy. If the class agrees that what the person says is merciful, they all take one small step forward. Then the person who has the ball tosses it to another person, and that person must come up with another way to show mercy.

If the class thinks that what the person says does not show mercy (you are the final judge), then everyone must take one step backward. If a person can't think of an answer, everyone stays in place. Continue until the circle is as small as you can make it. The point of the game is to get everyone to the center as quickly as possible.

Ask: What does being merciful to others achieve? *(It brings us closer together.)* **What does the opposite of mercy achieve?** *(It separates us.)*

DEPART   Time: 5 minutes

Say: All of us mess up, and when we do, we want mercy. But when somebody messes us up, we want justice! Do you see now what Jesus is showing us? If we are going to move ahead in life, there has to be mercy for everyone.

Together repeat the "Affirmation of Us."

Ask everyone to sit in silence and think of any way they may have done wrong this past week. After thirty seconds ask them to think of anyone who may have done something wrong to them this past week. After another thirty seconds of silence, pray.

Pray: All Merciful God, please forgive all of those things that I have done wrong this week. Please have mercy upon me. Give me the courage in my heart to forgive and show mercy to all those who need my forgiveness. Amen.

Mercy: The Love You Cannot Earn

Stuff—Mercy Ball:

❑ ball (beach ball)

Examples of showing mercy:
• not teasing a sister about whom she likes.
• forgiving someone who has been mean to you.
• not yelling back at someone who yells at you.
• saying, "I still like you" to a friend who has been unkind.
• doing the dishes without complaining when it was your brother's turn.
• taking out the trash in the rain when you sister is sick, even though it's her turn.

Stuff—Depart:

❑ "Affirmation of Us" poster, p. 64

Teacher Tip: Continue to follow up on the plans for your service project. Take whatever step is necessary this week and make sure that everyone has an assignment.

(Read page 60 for suggestions on how to start up and carry out a service project for your class.)

You will need to keep some time each week for checking on what's happening with your service project.

PLAN PLUS Time: 10-15 minutes

If you have extra time, you can try this "Mercy Inventory." Give the tweens sheets of paper and ask each one to write or draw a picture about the biggest injury or injustice done to him or her. Tell the tweens to turn their paper face down and join together in a worship circle.

Now, help your tweens enter into a spirit of meditation. **Say:**

1. Close your eyes and breathe slowly and deeply.

2. Relax your whole body, starting with your toes and working up to your eyes, forehead, and mind.

3. Visualize the scene of the injury or injustice done to you. Visualize the details. What kind of light is there? What smells are there? What tones of voice do you hear?

4. Visualize your own feelings. See them as a color: red hot? jealous green? hopeless blue? black despair? See the color deep inside yourself.

5. Now see Jesus sitting or standing next to you. Feel his hands on your head. Feel the light of the Holy Spirit filling your body. See the Light pouring into the dark color inside yourself. See the color of your hurt turning paler, paler, then disappearing as the Light continues to pour into you. Feel yourself filled with the Light of God.

6. Now look at the person or the thing that has hurt you. How do they look to you now, filled as you are with the Light of God?

7. Pray the same light for them. See the Light pour out on them, fill them, heal them.

8. Look at Jesus. Talk to him. What do you say? Does he answer? Listen.

9. It is time to end the meditation. Slowly count from ten to zero, then open your eyes.

Look back to your sheet of paper.

Ask: Is there any way you would change it?

Live It! Making a World of Difference

Reproducible 3A

The Unforgiving Servant

NARRATOR: There was a king who had loaned out some money to his servants. He decided things had gotten out of hand and it was time for the debts to be paid, so he called in Servant Number 1.

SERVANT NUMBER 1: *(bowing)* My king, you called for me?

KING: Yes, you owe me 10,000 talents, and as you know that's quite a lot of money. I am calling in the loan. I expect payment today.

SERVANT NUMBER 1: I don't have that kind of money right now. Perhaps in a few weeks?

KING: You know the law. Bailiff, he can't pay me. Confiscate everything he owns, and sell his wife and children. Bring the proceeds to me.

NARRATOR: Kings used to be able to do that sort of thing.

SERVANT NUMBER 1: My king! I know I have been very foolish and squandered my money without repaying my debts. But I beg of you, please forgive me. My wife and children have done nothing, and we all promise to work harder and start making payments right away! Oh please, I beg for mercy.

NARRATOR: The king was moved by the servant's tears and pleas for mercy.

KING: All right. Since you have asked for forgiveness, I will show you some mercy. You don't deserve it, but perhaps since you seem so earnest in your pleading you really mean it. You have spoken to my heart. I forgive your debt. You do not even have to repay what you owe. Go and be with your family.

SERVANT NUMBER 1: Thank you, my king. I'll never forget your graciousness and mercy.

NARRATOR: So Servant Number 1 left the king's palace full of rejoicing, but about that promise never to forget the king's mercy, well, that didn't last very long. As he left the palace, Servant Number 1 ran into Servant Number 2, who just happened to owe money to Servant Number 1.

SERVANT NUMBER 1: Servant Number 2, you owe me a hundred denarii, and I need you to pay it to me right now!

NARRATOR: A hundred denarii wasn't much; it was about one day's wages.

SERVANT NUMBER 2: Oh please have patience with me, and I will pay you.

SERVANT NUMBER 1: You are a thief if you don't pay your debts. Oh officer, I need some help here. I need to take this deadbeat to the debtor's prison.

NARRATOR: Servant Number 1 didn't learn his lesson from the king, but he's about to, for some other servants overheard what he did.

SERVANT NUMBER 3: Our king! Servant Number 1 had Servant Number 2 thrown in prison because he couldn't immediately pay him a hundred denarii.

SERVANT NUMBER 4: We don't think that's right, even if it is the law. Especially after what you did for him!

NARRATOR: The king became angry and had Servant Number 1 brought to him.

KING: You wicked slave! I forgave you all that debt because you pleaded with me. Should you not have had mercy on your fellow slave, as I had mercy on you?

NARRATOR: Servant Number 1 was punished very harshly for his lack of mercy, and he had to repay his entire debt. What do you think Jesus was trying to tell us through this parable?

Based on Matthew 18:23-34

Reproducible 3B

Scripture Phrase Cards

Stop being	bitter and angry	and
mad at others.	Don't yell	at one another
or	curse each other	or ever be rude.
Instead,	be kind	and merciful,
and forgive others,	just as	God
forgave you	because of	Christ.
Do as	God does.	After all,
you are his	dear children.	Let love
be	your guide.	(Ephesians 4:31–5:2a, CEV)

STEWARDS FOR GOD

THE POINT

God entrusted humankind with a unique task: to be stewards of all creation, and to ensure that the world God created continued to function as intended.

THE SKILLS

Tweens will:
• learn to connect their choices with being faithful to God's will for God's world.

THE BIBLE

Psalm 8; Psalm 24:1-2; Genesis 1:26

THE PLAN

PREPARE yourself

We often look at the human relationship to creation in one of two ways. Either we go with Genesis 1:26, which tells us that God gave us dominion (which is translated as domination over) all that is in the earth; or we take the Psalm 24:1 thought, which is, "The earth is the LORD's and all that is in it," and therefore we have no right to eat animals, or even wear clothes made from animals—some even say we shouldn't wear cotton from sheep.

PREPARE your session

Stuff to collect:

❏ NRSV Bibles
❏ items for the tweens to care for during the entire session, such as stuffed animals, dolls, eggs, rubber balls, or paper cups filled with water
❏ tape or pushpins
❏ pencils, colored pencils, and markers
❏ scissors
❏ construction paper
❏ containers
❏ items to create obstacle course, such as chairs, tables, and boxes
❏ four pounds of trash—paper, metal, glass, plastic foam
❏ multiple trash bags
❏ gloves
❏ **"Affirmation of Us" poster, p. 64**
❏ **Reproducible 4A, p. 35**
❏ **Reproducible 4B, p. 36**

For ☀ *cool options*:
❏ clear adhesive paper

Stuff to do:
1. Make photocopies of Reproducibles 4A and 4B.

Biblically, we have to look at these two concepts as a whole. God created us and gave us dominion, but the word *dominion* doesn't mean that we own creation and that we replace God, but rather that we are God's stewards here on earth, to care for and use creation. While we are caring for creation, we would be well-advised to remember that "The earth is the Lord's," and we are but the caretakers and the recipients of its benefits.

All of the images of sheep in the Bible tell us a lot about our relationship to the earth. Sheep were to be taken care of and treasured; even one lost lamb was to be searched for. Also sheep were used as a valuable part of the economy. They provided wool for clothing and they provided meat to sustain life. And originally they were used in animal sacrifice to God, offering God the first and best of what God had blessed humankind with. Not only this, but the blood of the lamb is what saved the Israelites from the death of their first born during the plagues on Egypt, and it is Jesus' sacrifice as the Lamb of God that brings us back into reconciliation with God.

There are many people in the Bible who give us hints as to what God meant by good stewardship of God's earth and everything in it (see the "Good Stewardship" cards, **Reproducible 4B, p. 36**).

Help your tweens understand that God gave us the earth to help sustain our lives and for our enjoyment. But in return, God gave us the responsibility over that creation to care for it for the sake of all creation. That includes all of humankind, as all people also belong to God and are not ours to abuse or treat wrongly.

GATHER

Practicing Dominion Time: entire session

As your tweens arrive, give them an object to care for during the entire session. They are to be the steward (caregiver) of this item for the entire session. The item is not to be left alone and must be with them and in good condition until they place it on the worship table at the end of the session.

Possible items include: stuffed animals, dolls, eggs, rubber balls, paper cups filled with water, or any items readily available to you.

This activity is a way to demonstrate the meaning of dominion through actions.

Stuff–Practicing Dominion:

☐ items for the tweens to care for during the entire session, such as stuffed animals, dolls, eggs, rubber balls, or paper cups filled with water

"The Earth Is the Lord's" Bookmark
Time: 5-10 minutes

Remind your tweens not to neglect nor forget the item given into their care as they do this activity. Give each tween a photocopy of "The Earth Is the Lord's" Bookmark (**Reproducible 4A, p. 35**). Tell them that they will be making a bookmark for their Bibles. Explain that the globe on the bookmark represents the world. Ask them to draw on the globe (or they may write words) a symbol(s) or image(s) of what God's world means to them. These can be detailed or abstract. The bookmark is for themselves. They can do this in colored pencil or do it first in plain pencil and then color in with markers or crayons.

Have brightly colored construction paper available. Let them choose a color, place their bookmark on the construction paper, and mark the edges so that their construction paper will be visible around the edges of the bookmark. Have them cut out the construction paper bookmark and glue the bookmark to it (or they may glue the bookmark on the paper first and then cut it out).

Stewardship Talk Time: 2-4 minutes

Explain that a *steward* is someone who takes care of something while the real owner is away. Let tweens describe something or someone they "steward." This might be a younger brother or sister, a pet, a garden, a lawn, and so forth.

INTERACT

Genesis 1:26 Time: 3-6 minutes

Say: The world was created by God and everything in it is important and a gift. And of all God's creations, the one creation unlike any other is the creation of you and me. Let's read about the role God has for us in all creation. Have tweens read Genesis 1:26 aloud together.

Introduce the word *dominion* and if necessary explain how it relates to good stewardship.

Ask: When God gives human beings dominion over all creation, who is intended to benefit? Are human beings meant to use creation in whatever manner suits them? Or is there some responsibility involved? *(God sees that "everything" God*

Stuff—"The Earth Is the Lord's" Bookmark:

❏ NRSV Bibles

❏ pencils, colored pencils, and markers

❏ scissors

❏ construction paper

❏ **Reproducible 4A, p. 35**

❏ *cool options:* clear adhesive paper

Cool Option: Use clear adhesive paper to have them laminate their bookmarks.

Stuff—Stewardship Talk:

❏ none

Teacher Tip: The "Stewardship Talk" activity would make a great conversation to have while the tweens are making bookmarks.

Stuff—Genesis 1:26:

❏ NRSV Bibles

"Who Am I?" Relay Race   Time: 10-15 minutes

Divide your tweens into small groups. Before class make two or more photocopies (depending upon class size) of the "Who Am I? Cards" (**Reproducible 4B, p. 36**) and cut them apart. Mix up each set of the cards and place each set in separate containers. Give each team a pencil and a Bible.

Have them line up as teams for a relay race. (Remind them that each person must carry the item for which he or she is acting as steward.) At your signal, the first person at the front of the line on each team races to their set of cards, pulls one card out and races back. That persons runs to the back of the line and hands the card to the last person in line. The last person in the line answers the riddle by writing a name on the card. If that person is stumped, he or she may ask help from the person who brought the riddle and/or from the rest of the team. The second person becomes the first person in line and he or she runs for the next card as soon as the answer is written on the first card. Proceed in this fashion until all the cards have been drawn and the riddle on each is solved.

The team that finishes first will read off their answers as you read each riddle. If they are incorrect on any riddle, other teams may read what they put down. If no one has it correct, read the biblical reference included in the answers below and let them race to look up the passage of Scripture and discover the true answer. Whoever gets to it first should shout out the answer.

Answers—"Who Am I?" Riddles
• We were given dominion over all things on earth. (*Humankind, Genesis 1:26*)
• I was given the responsibility of saving all of the animals from a great flood. (*Noah, Genesis 7:1-5*)
• I helped a nation prepare a food supply that would get them through a seven-year drought. (*Joseph, Genesis 41*)
• I gleaned leftover grain from the fields to feed my mother-in-law and myself. This also kept grain from going to waste. (*Ruth, Ruth 2:17*)
• We were just doing our job, taking care of the sheep, and God rewarded us by making us the first ones to hear the news of the birth of the Messiah. (*shepherds, Luke 2:8-20*)

Stuff–"Who Am I?" Relay Race:

❏ NRSV Bibles

❏ scissors

❏ pens or pencils

❏ containers

❏ **Reproducible 4B, p. 36**

Teacher Tip: If you have a small class, let them run the race as individuals.

Live It! Making a World of Difference

• After Jesus' resurrection, I was given the job of taking care of the faithful. *(Simon Peter, John 21:15-19)*
• We were chosen by the early church to make sure that food was distributed to those in need. *(seven chosen to serve–Stephen, Philip, Prochorus, Nicanor, Timon, Parmenas, and Nicolaus, Acts 6:1-7)*
• I was a Christian devoted to good works and acts of charity. Peter prayed over me, and I was raised from the dead. *(Tabitha/Dorcas, Acts 9:36-43)*

Good Stewardship Match Game Time: 10-15 minutes

Before class make nine signs on construction paper, with one of the following categories on each sign:

• birds
• fish
• trees
• plants
• insects
• people
• water
• air
• animals

Post the signs around the room.

Make one photocopy of the "Good Stewardship" cards **(Reproducible 4B, p. 36)**. Cut the cards apart, mix them up, and put them in a container.

Ask your tweens to look at the "Who Am I?" cards that they used in the "'Who Am I?' Relay Race" activity to see the types of things people in the Bible did to care for God's creation.
Say: These are just a few of the ways we can be good stewards of God's creation. Let's look at some more.

Explain that you have posted categories around the room. You will ask a volunteer (a different one each time) to pull one of the "Good Stewardship" cards out of the container and that person will read aloud what it says. As quickly as possible (and still taking care of the item they were entrusted with at the beginning of the session), all tweens in the class are to move to the category that they think the action would help take care of. Discuss the results.

Proceed with play until all cards have been used.

Stewards for God

Stuff–Good Stewardship Match Game:

☐ construction paper

☐ markers

☐ scissors

☐ tape or pushpins

☐ container

☐ **Reproducible 4B, p. 36**

Stuff:

☐ NRSV Bibles

☐ bookmarks made in "'The Earth Is the Lord's' Bookmark" activity

☐ **"Affirmation of Us" poster, p. 64**

Stuff—Obstacle Course:

☐ items to create obstacle course, such as chairs, tables, and boxes

Cool Option: On each item in the obstacle course pin a label, such as "medical waste," "oil spill," or "disrespect of a person."

Stuff—Four Pounds of Trash:

☐ NRSV Bibles

☐ four pounds of trash—paper, metal, glass, plastic foam

☐ multiple trash bags

☐ gloves

Teacher Tip: Continue to work on plans for your ongoing service project.

DEPART Time: 5 minutes

Gather the tweens around your worship table, each one carrying the object they have cared for and the Bible bookmarks they made at the beginning of the session.

Say: God has created us to be stewards over all creation. Ask your tweens to bring forward one at a time their cared-for item and place it on the worship table as you read aloud Psalm 8.

Together read the "Affirmation of Us." Then read Psalm 24:1 from the bookmarks they made. Close with the Lord's Prayer.

PLAN PLUS

Obstacle Course Time: 10 to 15 minutes

To make it difficult for tweens to care for their items, set up an obstacle course around a large room or outside area. Each tween must complete the course with their item still intact. Anyone who drops his or her item must start over. If any damage occurs to the item, he or she will be out. By necessity, the objective of this game is to complete the course successfully without damaging the item, not to be the fastest.

Four Pounds of Trash Time: 5 to 10 minutes

Before class collect and weigh out exactly four pounds of trash: paper, plastic, metal, glass, and plastic foam. If your state has a bottle bill, make sure there is a can or bottle with a deposit included. Whether or not your town has a recycling program, make sure your collection includes plastics that carry the "Recyclable" symbol. Prepare an area in which you can safely dump the trash.

Ask: How much trash does the average American create every day? Allow responses. Dump your bag of trash in your prepared area. **Say: The answer is four pounds.**

Say: You have four minutes to separate this trash into two piles. One pile will be for trash that was necessary, could not have been recycled, and could not have been used again. The other pile will be for trash that wasn't necessary, could have been recycled, or could have been used again. Go!

After four minutes, have them look at the trash piles while you read Psalm 8. Have them pick up the trash and put it in separate bags that you have provided. Together have them read Psalm 24:1.

Live It! Making a World of Difference

The earth is
the LORD's
and all that is
in it, the world,
and those who
live in it.
(Psalm 24:1)

The earth is
the LORD's
and all that is
in it, the world,
and those who
live in it.
(Psalm 24:1)

The earth is
the LORD's
and all that is
in it, the world,
and those who
live in it.
(Psalm 24:1)

Art: Dennis Jones

Who Am I? Cards	Good Stewardship Cards
We were given dominion over all things on earth.	Give clothes you have outgrown to a charity or thrift store.
I was given the responsibility of saving all of the animals from a great flood.	Recycle all old papers and magazines.
I helped a nation prepare a food supply that would get them through a seven-year drought.	Never smoke a cigarette.
	Treat other people with respect.
I gleaned leftover grain from the fields to feed my mother-in-law and myself. This also kept grain from going to waste.	Use a lunch box or cloth lunch bag instead of a disposable bag.
	Keep room clean.
We were just doing our job, taking care of the sheep, and God rewarded us by making us the first ones to hear the news of the birth of the Messiah.	Learn everything possible about the rain forests and pass the information along.
After Jesus' resurrection I was given the job of taking care of the faithful.	Pray for peace in the world.
	Have a yard sale.
We were chosen by the early church to make sure that food was distributed to those in need.	Ride your bicycle instead of using a car.
I was a Christian devoted to good works and acts of charity. Peter prayed over me, and I was raised from the dead.	Plant a tree.
	Learn natural ways to get rid of unwanted insects.

YOUR MISSION, YOUR GIFTS

THE POINT

As Christians we are all members of the body of the church, and therefore we are called to the mission of the church (spreading the good news of the love of God through Jesus Christ). Through the Holy Spirit we are all given gifts that help us carry out our part of the mission.

THE SKILLS

Tweens will:
• learn that mission means sharing faith, setting a good example, and using our gifts for God's glory and the greater good of all.
• begin discovering their gifts for missions.

THE BIBLE

Matthew 28:19-20; 1 Corinthians 12:4-6, 12-26

THE PLAN

PREPARE yourself

Matthew 28:19-20 is called the Great Commission. Since Jesus would no longer be with the disciples physically, he passed the stewardship of the good news of God's saving grace to them.

Without the Great Commission, the body of Christ, the church, would never have been spread. Indeed it would have been quite a small group if everyone was required to have the same skills.

PREPARE your session

Stuff to collect:

❏ NRSV Bibles
❏ pens or pencils
❏ scissors
❏ paper
❏ card stock, posterboard, or art board
❏ markers
❏ CD of Christian music
❏ CD player
❏ **"Affirmation of Us" poster, p. 64**
❏ **Reproducible 5A, p. 43**
❏ **Reproducible 5B, p. 44**

Stuff to do:
1. Make photocopies of Reproducibles 5A and 5B.

However, the Holy Spirit was sent to the early church. To help us understand, **1 Corinthians 12:26** explains that we are all part of the body of Christ. In fact **1 Corinthians 12:4-6** says, "There are varieties of gifts, but the same Spirit; and there are varieties of services, but the same Lord; and there are varieties of activities, but it is the same God who activates all of them in everyone."

In this session help your tweens begin to understand that they too are called to be active, participating members of the church (both local and universal), and that they will be given gifts to carry out what they are called to do.

Sometimes a person is called to a lifetime of mission in one way and one area; others are given specific tasks (and the gifts to match) for specific periods of time, and those tasks can change as the world around them changes. And yes, sometimes we are asked to go through periods of preparation for our mission. Remember the disciples required a lot of teaching and living with Jesus' example, and they still needed the death and the Resurrection before they "got it."

Today's session asks your tweens to stretch themselves and their maturity level. Don't worry if their answers are not as deep as you would like. You are planting the seeds for further spiritual growth.

GATHER

Mission Survival! Time: 10 minutes

As tweens arrive give each a copy of "Survival Test" **(Reproducible 5A, top of p. 43)** and a pencil. Ask the tweens to read the instructions and begin to work on the task.

As others arrive encourage them to work together to complete the task. If you have more than seven or eight tweens, begin to divide them into small groups to work, dividing them by arrival times.

Once everyone has arrived, call the groups together and see if they were able to divide up the tasks.

Stuff–Mission Survival!:

❏ pens or pencils

❏ **Reproducible 5A, p. 43**

Teacher Tip: Be sure to cut off the Roleplay Cards at the bottom of Reproducible 5A. Save them to be used in the "It Takes All Kinds of Disciples" activity.

Live It! Making a World of Difference

INTERACT

Mission's the Word   Time: 5-10 minutes

Say: The word *mission* **means "to be sent." I can send you on a mission to get us a pitcher of water, or the mission can be something bigger.** Ask a tween to read Matthew 28:18-20.

Say: The disciples were given a mission. We often equate a mission with a "service project."

Ask: Does anyone know the difference between a service project and a mission project? *(A service project is any good work of service; a mission project is one that is taken on because we are sent by Christ into the world. It usually contains the element of taking or being the good news of the Gospel to someone.)*

Ask: When you hear about "a mission project" at church, what comes to mind? Allow time for response. If for some reason your church does not engage in mission projects, be ready to give examples from other congregations: food pantries, soup kitchens, homeless shelters, medical clinics, mentoring programs, prison visitation programs, supporting missionaries, supporting mission projects for building things in other places, and so forth.

Say: All of these are wonderful. They help us to grow in awareness of the world around us and how we can make a positive impact on the lives of others. They help us to accomplish our main goal, which is to be the good news for all people. But what about your special mission? Your life mission? The mission that you were born for? Most people don't know right away what that is.

It Takes All Kinds of Disciples   Time: 10-15 minutes

Make a photocopy of the roleplay cards (**Reproducible 5A, bottom of p. 43**). Cut the cards apart and mix them up. Divide the class into small teams. Let each team draw one of the roleplay cards. Let them have three minutes to prepare their roleplays and then let each team present their roleplay.

Talk about what kinds of gifts are required to deal with the needs in each roleplay.

Teacher Tip: It is not necessary to use all of the roleplays for them to get the point of the exercise.

Many Members   Time: 15-20 minutes

Ask your tweens to remember the "Mission Survival!" activity they completed when they came in. Talk about how no one could do all of the tasks; everyone was needed and a variety of different skills were required.

Ask a tween to volunteer to read 1 Corinthians 12:4. Pass out photocopies of **Reproducible 5B, p. 44**. Take turns letting tweens read the different tasks listed under "It's What Disciples Do."

Say: Everybody can do parts of the tasks, but all of us are needed to complete the tasks—for example, all disciples are called on to worship and to perform service, but somebody has to prepare and lead the worship experience. All disciples are called on to do service, but there are so many types of service, we would not accomplish anything if we all did the same thing.

Ask a tween to read 1 Corinthians 12:14.

Divide your tweens into the groups they were in for the Gather activities and tell them they are now going to do the same type of work as they did on the "Mission Survival!" activity at the beginning of the session, only this time their group is going to be starting a new church. For the church to survive and do the work of discipleship required of all churches, they will need many talents. Ask them to look at "Discipleship Gifts" on **Reproducible 5B** to see what gifts would be helpful in their new church. Give them five minutes to decide who in your class might have which talents to help in the different areas the church must address in order to survive.

Make "Gifts" Posters   Time: 8-10 minutes

Give each tween a piece of card stock, posterboard, or art board (size depends upon number of tweens in your group) and some colorful markers.

Ask each tween to write his or her name in large letters colorfully and decoratively in the middle of his or her poster. Tell tweens that they have been studying the gifts needed for the church to carry on its mission in the world. Now it is time to "discern" gifts in each other. Perhaps they are not even the gifts you have talked specifically about yet; maybe they are things like writing, playing music, or just having the ability to make people feel good.

Live It! Making a World of Difference

Have each person place his or her poster on a table or tables around the room. Tell the tweens that you are going to play some music and while it is playing each person in the room is to write on the poster of all the others one gift they see in that person. They are to write on each poster, and it must be a positive gift. If they need a little help, you will be there to help them find the right words to say what they mean.

Play a CD of your favorite Christian music or one song that you feel particularly fits the mood.

You will need to monitor this activity to ensure everyone signs all the posters. Gather the posters yourself when everyone is finished.

DEPART Time: 5-7 minutes

Place the posters on the worship table and gather the tweens there. Together repeat the "Affirmation of Us." Ask one of the tweens to read aloud 1 Corinthians 12:4.

Ask the tweens to come forward, take their own posters, and return to their seats. It will be more orderly if you read out the name on the top poster and then the name on each subsequent poster. This will keep them from having to hunt through the pile.

As each tween picks up his or her poster, **Say: Thanks be to God for the gifts of {tween's name}.**

When finished, **Pray: Almighty God, thank you for the gifts we have been given so that we can serve you better. Help us go this week and help us use our gifts wherever we may be. Amen.**

Stuff-Depart:

❏ NRSV Bibles

❏ **"Affirmation of Us" poster, p. 64**

PLAN PLUS

❑ none

Teacher Tip: You might wish to do this activity before they do the "Make 'Gifts' Posters" activity.

Gifts for Now Time: 8-10 minutes

Explain to tweens that spiritual gifts are given to us to fit the lives that we are living now, and as our needs change and develop so may our spiritual gifts.

To help tweens discover what they are each meant to be doing for God right now in their everyday lives, read the situations below and as a class have them discuss what outcome they would like the situation to have. Brainstorm what kinds of gifts some people their age might have that are needed for this situation.

Situation One: One of the kids in your class tells you that she is e-mailing somebody she's never met who is very interesting, but she doesn't want her parents to find out.

Situation Two: Kids at school talk about cheating a lot like it's no big deal. You have been taught in Sunday school that cheating is always wrong. You don't cheat, but you don't want to be seen as a nerd.

Situation Three: One of your classmates is Muslim. He has told you something about his beliefs. He asks what Christians believe.

Situation Four: There is going to be an election for class president. You don't like some of the things that have been happening at school. You feel that if someone with the same values as you got elected, things would be better.

Continue Service Project

Continue with your service project. You may wish today to check and see if your tweens would like to add or perhaps switch responsibilities after looking at their gifts.

Stuff–Continue Service Project:

❑ none

42

Reproducible 5A

Survival Test

Imagine that your class is marooned on a tropical island. It is your job to think about the special gifts and talents of each person in your class and give to them a mission that will help the whole class to survive.

You are allowed to equip each of your classmates with the tools he or she will need to accomplish his or her task (but remember, there aren't any electric outlets on a desert island!).

The tasks to be accomplished include:

1. Building a shelter.
2. Devising and constructing a rescue signal.
3. Finding and preparing food.
4. Keeping up everyone's spirits.
5. Setting up rules of behavior and keeping the community in harmony.
6. Prayer.

Roleplay Cards

It's Sunday morning at New Hope Church. They are having a rough time because the flu has struck and several key people are missing this morning. The liturgist (one who reads the Scripture, the announcements, and so forth), the choir director, and one of the ushers all called in sick, and the church secretary was so sick that there was no one to do the worship bulletin.

New Hope Church had a burglary Saturday night. The burglar left several of the classrooms all messed up with toys, chairs, and papers thrown all over the place.

There's been a fire in an apartment building close to your church.

There's been a devastating earthquake in a country halfway around the world.

There's a new kid in your school. She seems to be having a hard time making friends.

One of your friends says he doesn't believe in God.

It's What Disciples Do

Disciples of Jesus…

Witness to the world about what Jesus has done for them in their lives by what they say and how they live.

Invite others to come and experience the love of Jesus through the community of the church. (This witnessing and inviting can be as complex as a multimillion dollar media campaign, or as simple as a phone call to a friend.)

Practice faithfulness and "recharge" their spiritual lives through worship, prayer, and service. (By inviting others to share this experience, they may get "charged up" themselves.)

Live out their Christian mission in all types of service to others.

Work for the good of all everywhere, for all are children of God. Advocate for those who have no power of their own.

Discipleship Gifts

1. Apostles (missionaries) are those sent out to spread the gospel to new places and to new people.

2. Prophets speak the truth boldly, proclaiming justice and defending the poor.

3. Teachers pass on the wisdom of the faith to others.

4. Miracle Workers:
   • Those given the rare gift of performing miracles.
   • Those who are the generous.
   • Those who sacrifice for the good of others.
   • Those who help others see the power and glory of God.

5. Healers:
   • Doctors and nurses who have studied for years to use the knowledge they gain of God's creation to heal the sick.
   • Scientists who use God's creation to discover ways to heal people.
   • People who pray for the sick.
   • Comforters and caregivers
   • Spiritual Healers who bring comfort to the spiritually sick.
   • People who sit with the sick.

6. Servers:
   • Those who build or repair things that are needed.
   • Those who give financial assistance.
   • Those who volunteer time and talents.

7. Leaders:
   • In worship.
   • In service.
   • In any way that leads others to God and to God's work on earth.

THE POINT

God's world was created to live in peace; each of us needs to be participants in helping to bring and maintain peace on God's earth.

THE SKILLS

Tweens will:
• think about what living peaceably together means.
• practice cooperative participation in activities.

THE BIBLE

Matthew 5:9; Numbers 6:24-26; Micah 4:3-4; Psalm 37:37; Romans 12:18; 1 Corinthians 14:33

THE PLAN

PREPARE yourself

The Bible talks a lot about living peacefully together. God's kingdom was created to be peaceful, but ever since Adam and Eve first tasted the forbidden fruit, envy, jealousy, greed, hatred, and sin have brought war and discord to God's people. This is not a state that God wishes us to continue to live in.

However, the peace talked about is not a false peace, that is an absence of war, but a true peace that can come only from living as

PREPARE your session

Stuff to collect:

- ☐ NRSV Bibles
- ☐ pens or pencils
- ☐ construction paper
- ☐ markers
- ☐ masking tape
- ☐ white paper
- ☐ foil paper
- ☐ scissors
- ☐ glue
- ☐ glitter
- ☐ paper bags
- ☐ watch or timer
- ☐ aluminum cans or plastic soda containers
- ☐ ribbon and/or yarn
- ☐ large sheet of paper or posterboard
- ☐ camera and film
- ☐ bulletin board
- ☐ items required to complete service project
- ☐ *optional:* items to decorate bulletin board
- ☐ **"Affirmation of Us" poster, p. 64**
- ☐ **Reproducible 6A, p. 51**
- ☐ **Reproducible 6B, p. 52**

Stuff to do:

1. Make photocopies of Reproducibles 6A and 6B.

a true child of God. Even families will be divided if some turn to God and others turn away from God. Sound like any households you know?

Today's session cannot deal with all facets of peace, so we will deal with equipping tweens to begin to see themselves as peacemakers, as all disciples should be. In order to bring peace to the world, we must change how we relate to each other and the world.

Tweens, like all of us, must first learn to live with those around them. Nevertheless, tweens are at an age when they can step onto a larger stage as peacemakers. It is a good time to introduce tweens to making a more peaceful world, as this is a time that they take an interest in effecting change in the world.

The Beatitudes tell us "Blessed are the peacemakers, for they will be called children of God" (**Matthew 5:9**). Does this not tell us that to be in right relationship with God, we need to, as much as possible within our control, live in peace with others?

Tweens need to learn patterns of thinking about how to live righteously in God's world. That is the only thing that will enable them to actually live righteously in God's world.

To help your tweens model more peaceful behavior, a peaceful classroom setting needs to be developed. How are arguments settled in the classroom? Do your tweens ever work together cooperatively, or is everything a competition? Do you rotate groups so that tweens don't develop cliques and so that they learn how to develop relationships with many people?

Even competition can be used to help develop a peaceful classroom atmosphere. "Winning at all costs" is never appropriate in a Christ-centered classroom. Conversely, "it's not whether you win or lose, but how you play the game" is the centerpiece to peaceful competition.

Live It! Making a World of Difference

GATHER

Peaceful Acrostic Time: 3-4 minutes

Before class make photocopies of the Peaceful Acrostic puzzle (**Reproducible 6A, p. 51**). As tweens arrive have them work the puzzle.

Answer:
    P r a y
    l **E** ar n
    te **A** c h
    parti **C** i p a t e
    beli **E** v e

Make Up Peaceful Names Time: 3-8 minutes

As they finish their acrostic, give each tween a piece of construction paper and a marker.

Say: You have already figured out today's session is about peace. People who truly know each other well and understand each other are more likely to treat each other well.

Ask the tweens to think of a nickname for themselves that will tell others something about who they are, then write that nickname in big letters on the construction paper. Have them tape the name to their shirt fronts with masking tape. This is their "oversized" nametag for the day.

After all have gathered, let each explain why he or she chose that specific nickname.

INTERACT

Bible Scavenger Hunt Time 25-30 minutes

Before class prepare "Bible Scavenger Hunt Kits" for each group in your class. There are six Bible Scavenger Hunt Cards (**Reproducible 6B, p. 52**). Make a photocopy of the cards, cut them apart, and put each in a paper bag along with the other items that go in the specific kit (see list of kit contents on the next page).

Before the first tween arrives, hide the kits around the classroom or larger area of the church if possible.

Stuff–Peaceful Acrostic:

- [ ] pens or pencils
- [ ] **Reproducible 6A, p. 51**

Stuff–Make Up Peaceful Names:

- [ ] construction paper
- [ ] markers
- [ ] masking tape

Stuff–Bible Scavenger Hunt:

- [ ] NRSV Bibles
- [ ] white paper
- [ ] construction paper
- [ ] pencils
- [ ] markers
- [ ] paper bags
- [ ] foil paper
- [ ] scissors
- [ ] glue
- [ ] glitter
- [ ] aluminum cans or plastic soda containers
- [ ] ribbon and/or yarn
- [ ] large sheet of paper
- [ ] **Reproducible 6B, p. 52**

Cool Option: If short on space, time, or tweens, use the Scriptures listed on the Bible Scavenger Hunt Cards (**Reproducible 6B**) to send them racing through their Bibles to find the passage of Scripture and read it aloud.

Teacher Tip: If the tweens have to leave the room to find their kits, have a set time by which they are to return to the area.

Divide your class into teams (up to six teams). If you have a very large class, make more than one set of kits.

Send your tweens out by teams to find a kit. They must use the first kit they find. As soon as they find the kit, they are to work as a team to read their passage of Scripture and follow the directions.

Once every team has found a kit and completed the required tasks, gather them in a group. Give them five minutes to prepare a presentation to the entire class based on their kit.

At the end of the time allowed, bring all tweens back together. Have each team designate a reader. The reader will read the Scripture verses and then the group will quickly make their presentation.

The team that found kit 4 will keep their presentation until worship time, as their assignment is to read the passage of Scripture for worship. Be sure that all teams know this now so that team 4 does not feel left out.

Materials needed for each kit:

• *Kit 1:* Micah 4:3-4 card from **Reproducible 6B**, NRSV Bible, two pieces of white paper or construction paper, pencils, and markers.

• *Kit 2:* Matthew 5:9 card from **Reproducible 6B**, NRSV Bible, paper, construction paper, foil paper, scissors, markers, glue, glitter, items such as plastic soda containers or aluminum cans, ribbon, and/or yarn (anything that they might use to make an "award").

• *Kit 3:* Psalm 37:37 card from **Reproducible 6B**, NRSV Bible, large sheet of paper, and markers.

• *Kit 4:* Numbers 6:24-26 card from **Reproducible 6B** and several NRSV Bibles.

• *Kit 5:* 1 Corinthians 14:33 card from **Reproducible 6B** and NRSV Bible.

• *Kit 6:* Romans 12:18 card from **Reproducible 6B**, NRSV Bible, two or more colors of construction paper, markers, and glue.

Live It! Making a World of Difference

Cooperative Art Time: 10-12 minutes

Do a cooperative art project to help your tweens practice the process of working cooperatively instead of competitively. Divide the class into groups of five. Give each group a large sheet of paper or posterboard and some markers. Tell them that they will draw a group picture of their idea of a perfect, peaceful world.

First you will give them two minutes to decide what they want to draw. Tell them that you will say when they should begin to draw. Before they work together, tell them to think about these things:

- What kind of world do you want to draw—realistic, abstract, or a combination?
- Can that kind of picture be easily drawn?
- What are the different things you will draw?
- What part do you want to draw?

Let them use these questions during their two minutes to decide their assignments. At the end of the two minutes, call time. Tell them that you will be reading a Bible passage while they draw. Tell them to begin drawing, while you slowly and dramatically read Micah 4:3-4. Then in turn read Matthew 5:9, Psalm 37:37, Numbers 6:24-26, 1 Corinthians 14:33, and Romans 12:18, as many of these passages as are needed as they do their drawings. If you have read all the passages, and they have not completed their drawings, stop them anyway and bring them back together.

Ask them to talk about how they felt about the process.

Ask: Was it easy or hard to decide what to do? Was it easy or hard to work together without disagreement? How did you settle any disagreements? Did everyone contribute something?

DEPART Time: 5 minutes

Ask everyone to wear their nametags to the worship area (if they have taken them off). Together recite the "Affirmation of Us."

Have each tween remove his or her nametag and one at a time place it on the altar, **Saying: My name is _____ and I dedicate myself to making God's world peaceful.**

At this time have team 4 read the benediction they prepared earlier (Numbers 6:24-26).

Stuff–Cooperative Art:

- ❏ NRSV Bibles
- ❏ large sheet of paper or posterboard
- ❏ markers
- ❏ watch or timer

Stuff–Depart:

- ❏ NRSV Bibles
- ❏ **"Affirmation of Us" poster, p. 64**

PLAN PLUS

Body Spelling Bulletin Board Time: 5-20 minutes

How much time this activity will take this week will depend upon the kind of camera and film that is used. If film must be developed, you will have to take the pictures this week and make the actual bulletin board next week. If you have an instant camera, you can complete the activity this week.

Have five tweens at a time pose spelling out the word *peace* (see illustration below). You will need to take individual pictures of each letter for the bulletin board, but stand farther back and be sure to take a group picture of the five as well.

When the pictures are developed, have the tweens use them to make a bulletin board about peace. They may wish to use only their pictures, or they may wish to add things like folded cranes (symbols of peace), the peace symbol (made popular in the 1960s), or other decorations of some kind.

If you have more than five tweens they may want to use all the pictures to spell out the word *peace* vertically, horizontally, diagonally, and backward, as well as forward. Help them use their imaginations.

Stuff—Body Spelling Bulletin Board:

- ❑ camera and film

- ❑ bulletin board

- ❑ *optional:* items to decorate bulletin board

Teacher Tip: Check with your church to see if you can use a bulletin board that is in a prominent place so that others in the church can see it.

Art: Dennis Jones

Stuff—Service Project Finale

- ❑ items required to complete service project

Service Project Finale

If you have not already done so, you should be preparing to finish up or to carry out the service project you have been working on throughout these sessions. Review what you have done on the service project and why. Celebrate the completion of the project!

Live It! Making a World of Difference

P P _ _ _ _ _

_ _ E _ _ _ _ _

_ _ A _ _ _

_ _ _ _ _ C _ _ _ _ _ _ _ _

_ _ _ _ E _ _

Use the clues below to find the words that go in the acrostic.

Clue #1—Something we do when we need God's help or blessing.

Clue #2—Studying, reading, or exploring people and things in order to know more about them.

Clue #3—Tutoring someone or helping someone understand something that you already know.

Clue #4—To become part of things instead of just watching or criticizing.

Clue #5—To trust that something is possible, especially with the help of God.

Reproducible 6B

Bible Scavenger Hunt Cards

Read Micah 4:3-4.

Name two weapons that could be made into two peaceful (and useful) items. What would those peaceful items be? Write or draw these peaceful items.

Read Numbers 6:24-26.

Practice reading these verses together as you will read this passage as the closing prayer today.

Read Matthew 5:9.

Create an award to be given to a peacemaker.

Read 1 Corinthians 14:33.

Make up a pantomime of two ways to be peaceful in God's world. Practice to show others later.

Read Psalm 37:37.

Make a list of good things that happen when people learn to live peaceably together.

Read Romans 12:18.

Option 1: Draw two ways you can live more peaceably with those around you.
Option 2: Make a torn paper picture of a way you can live more peaceably with those around you. (Abstract art is okay.)

Live It! Making a World of Difference

TWEENS AND PARENTS TOGETHER

THE POINT

Families grow stronger as they make living righteously in God's world their central family value.

THE SKILLS

Tweens and parents will:
• practice working as a team.
• develop a family shalom project.

THE BIBLE

Genesis 1:26; Acts 6:1-7; 1 Corinthians 12:4-14

THE PLAN

PREPARE yourself

Families and churches have differences and similarities. While churches are voluntary organizations, families are more a matter of who your parents are. While we choose a marriage partner, we don't choose who our parents are, nor do we usually choose who our children are. (The exception is adoption.)

However, like churches, families must divide tasks to function in any meaningful way. Someone has to earn money, someone has to do the dishes, and someone has to feed the dog. Luckily, God has taken care of this. God has given us different gifts. Used for the

PREPARE your session

Stuff to collect:

- [ ] NRSV Bibles
- [ ] large sheets of paper
- [ ] markers
- [ ] basket or bag
- [ ] items for building, such as children's building blocks, plastic foam cups, masking tape, plastic cups, string or yarn, cardboard boxes
- [ ] watch or timer
- [ ] pens or pencils
- [ ] covered dishes for potluck supper (provided by families)
- [ ] disposable plates, napkins, cups, and utensils
- [ ] **"Affirmation of Us" poster, p. 64**
- [ ] **Reproducible 7A, p. 57**
- [ ] **Reproducible 7B, p. 58**

Stuff to do:
1. Make photocopies of Reproducibles 7A and 7B.

2. If you are having a meal as part of your class time, make sure parents and tweens know what to bring.

common good these gifts are a blessing to the whole body of the family. The same is true of the church.

On a much larger scale, the same is true of the world. God created the world and we were given dominion over this world **(Genesis 1:26),** and that dominion includes the responsibility of good stewardship of all of God's creation (each other included).

Once again, though, we are not alone. The gifts God has given us enable us to work together in a way that can make the world a better place. In order for the world to be better for all of us, we need to work together, each of us using our own gifts. The Holy Spirit brings us these gifts for a reason.

Today, work together as a church group and as family units to discover a way to help better the world God has given us stewardship over.

GATHER

We're Concerned About... Time: 5-7 minutes

As tweens and their parents arrive, have them sit as a group. Give each family a large sheet of paper and a marker.

Ask each family to come up with a list of things about the larger world that they are concerned about and/or interested in. Each family member needs to contribute something to the list.

Explain that the list is to be about what they think is important. The list can consist of everything from global warming, to terrorism, to planting flowers along the highway; it can include everything from people not being nice enough to each other, to babies with AIDS. Anything can be a concern, as long as the concern is very specific.

When all have gathered, have them post their lists around the room. It is very likely that all lists will not be the same. There are a lot of interests and a lot of tasks that need to be worked on.

Explain that they will come back to these lists later.

Stuff—We're Concerned About...:

❑ large sheets of paper

❑ markers

INTERACT

Bible Time Time: 15-20 minutes

Before the session ask two people who read well to prepare to read today's Bible passages.

Have the first reader read aloud Genesis 1:26. **Ask: Why do you think God gave dominion to people?** If no one mentions it, be prepared to talk about how God gave humans stewardship over the land. Dominion for God's people also implies good stewardship.

Ask the second reader to read Acts 6:1-7 immediately followed by third reader reading 1 Corinthians 12:4-7, 12. **Ask: What does this mean about our stewardship of all the earth?**

Tell them that they will spend the rest of the session learning to work together using their various talents.

Build It Time: 7-10 minutes

Have the families count off by fours or fives (depending upon how large your group is). You want some of all ages working in groups together, but for this activity don't put families together.

Tell them that they will quickly learn what some of their talents are by working together to build something. In a basket or a bag have an assortment of items for each group. Tell them they have five minutes to decide what to build and to build it. How they accomplish the task and what they build is up to each group.

Possible items for building:
• children's building blocks
• plastic foam cups and masking tape
• plastic cups and string or yarn
• cardboard boxes and masking tape

Tell them to start on their object and stop them at exactly five minutes. Let each team show what they have built.

Ask about who did what in the process. If most of the work was done by adults in any group, ask them why. Remind them that God has given gifts even to the young and that instead of doing things for them, we need to do things with them, letting them work according to their talents.

Tweens and Parents Together

Stuff–Bible Time:

❑ NRSV Bibles

Stuff–Build It:

❑ basket or bag

❑ items for building, such as children's building blocks, plastic foam cups, masking tape, plastic cups, string or yarn, cardboard boxes

❑ watch or timer

Teacher Tip: If you have only a short time, you may substitute the "Build It" activity for the "We're Concerned About…" activity. If you have a longer session, give them more time to do their building.

Cool Option: Give each team a different set of items for the building project.

Stuff–Family Project:

- [ ] pens or pencils

- [ ] **Reproducibles 7A and 7B, pp. 57-58**

Stuff–Depart:

- [ ] NRSV Bibles

- [ ] **Reproducible 7A and 7B, pp. 57-58**

- [ ] **"Affirmation of Us" poster, p. 64**

Stuff–Enjoy a Meal Together:

- [ ] covered dishes for potluck supper (provided by families)

- [ ] disposable plates, napkins, cups, and utensils

Family Project Time: 10-15 minutes

Say: God has given every church, every family, and every person a mission in life. God wants more beauty and more justice in God's world. The special mission for you and your family depends upon the special gifts and talents God has given each one of you. Where the needs of the world, and your talents, come together—that is where you will find your mission.

Say: Our last task in this class is for each family to find its own mission to promote peace, justice and/or beauty using the talents of all family members.

Pass out copies of "Family Project for a Better World" (**Reproducibles 7A and 7B, pp. 57-58**) to everyone present. Then have them gather in family units and follow the directions to come up with a family project.

DEPART Time: 5 minutes

Bring everyone together, asking them to bring their family plan (**Reproducibles 7A and 7B**). Ask them to sit together as families (or if families have teamed up to work on projects, ask them to sit together by project families).

Ask everyone to read the "Affirmation of Us" together.

Challenge the families to carry out their family project and to talk about the experience when the project is finished.

Read Numbers 6:24-26 as your closing prayer.

PLAN PLUS

Enjoy a Meal Together Time: 30-45 minutes

Each family should bring a covered dish to contribute to the dinner. Ask for volunteers for different tasks—setting the table, saying the blessing, clearing the table, doing the dishes if necessary, and sweeping up the floors.

Just be sure that no one misses any of the rest of the session.

Live It! Making a World of Difference

FAMILY PROJECT FOR A BETTER WORLD

1. What are the special gifts and talents of each member of your family, as you see them? Write down a time when you saw this gift or talent put into action.

FAMILY MEMBER	GIFTS AND TALENTS	WHEN SEEN USED

2. What kind of family project to promote peace, justice, and/or beauty would make best use of all these gifts and talents?

◆___ building or mechanical project

◆___ artistic, dramatic, or musical project

◆___ computer or research project

◆___ outdoor or gardening project

◆___ recreation or sports project

◆___ personal care-giving project

◆___ cooking or household project

◆___ fundraising or publicity project

◆___ writing project

◆___ spiritual, religious, or church project

◆___ another project

_____

_____

3. Stop and see if there are other families in the class with gifts and talents for the same kind of project. If so, decide if you want to share a project or do separate projects.

4. Set a challenging but achievable and measurable goal for your family project:

By _____ (date) we will accomplish this goal: _____

5. Assign each family member a task that will help accomplish this goal, using their unique gifts and talents.

NAME	Assignment	Date Completed

We covenant together to accomplish this task, helping to build the shalom (justice and beauty) of God.

_____   _____

_____   _____

_____   _____

_____   _____

Whom Shall I Send?

God expects all of us to be good stewards of God's creation. Listed on this page are some things that young people can volunteer to do related to specific issues or concerns. (There are many more options—talk with people from your church, your school, and local social service agencies for more ideas.)

✻ **The Earth:** Concerned about the environment? Many schools and towns support beautification programs. See if there is a roadside area or public building that needs a volunteer planting of flower bulbs, shrubs, or saplings. You will need adults to supervise this project. Earth Day and National Arbor Day, both in April, are especially appropriate for this kind of task.

Another option is to plant a tree in your yard and take care of it, or plant a butterfly garden in your yard and take care of it.

✻ **The Earth or People's Health**: Almost every organization appreciates preteens who can organize a fundraising project. Consider the many ways preteens have raised thousands of dollars for worthy causes: signing up sponsors for a walk, a climb, a swim, a run, or a biking trip; asking family members, neighbors, and friends to buy an item you either make yourself or buy wholesale; and offering your services for yard work or chores in exchange for a donation.

✻ **Justice:** Organizations such as Amnesty International and Bread for the World are constantly asking for people to write letters. Set a goal for writing a certain number of letters on behalf of a cause you care about. Information on these organizations can be found on the Internet; just be sure that you have their "official" site (*www.amnesty.org* and *www.bread.org*, for example).

✻ **People in Your Family**: Volunteer to stay with a sick grandparent while your parents run errands; help your younger brother or sister with some of his or her homework; play a game with a younger sibling that he or she likes (even if you don't like it); do family chores without having to be asked; try talking respectfully to other family members.

✻ **Church**: Sing in the children's or youth choir; help keep your classroom clean; treat your teacher and classmates with respect; help arrange chairs for a program; help with the church's volunteer programs whenever possible; tithe on your allowance.

✻ **Other Things to Do:** Donate gently used clothing, toys, books, and video games to a community center when you are done with them; learn to live on a budget and use your money wisely (this will enable you to help a lot of people, yourself included, in the future); discover what you are good at and ask for an adult to help you find how you can use your talent.

Service Project Helps

Set an ambitious but achievable goal for your group.

If you are going to do something for an existing agency, contact the agency to see what they need and in what form and how they will allow underaged children to be involved.

Ask for volunteers or assign tasks depending upon what needs to be done and the talents of your tweens.

- ➤ Will you be raising money? If so, what tasks will need to be performed?
- ➤ Will you be performing a service? If so, what tasks will need to be performed?
- ➤ What will be the time frame for your project? Will it be a one time thing or will it take multiple meetings and a longer period of time to complete?
- ➤ Do notes or permission forms need to be sent home?
- ➤ Will you need to do publicity work? If so, what kind, how much, and who will do it?
- ➤ How will you make sure that all tasks are on track and being performed?
- ➤ What will you do if someone doesn't do his or her task?

You may wish to involve your Faith Friends in the project along with the tweens. Remember that everyone must share equally in the work.

Some project possibilities:
- ✱ Plant trees or flowers for the church or some individual church members.
- ✱ Raise money for a project that affects children close to home or overseas.
- ✱ Pick a missionary to support with letters.
- ✱ Research information on a problem and use the church newsletter, Web site, and bulletin boards to educate others (permission from the church will be needed).
- ✱ Plan a trip to a nursing home. Prepare a program to present showcasing the talents of your tweens. Sit and talk with the patients before or after the program.

When the service project is completed, come back together and talk about the experience.

Parent and Tween Communication

Parents and tweens really want to communicate. Many of them just haven't figured out how to get the conversation started or how to keep it going. What's the hang-up? Fear—pure and simple.

Fear of what? Some fears are different for parents and tweens, and others are the same. Let's consider a few possibilities.

Sometimes parents fear
• being rejected by their tweens
• having the truth about their own youthful indiscretions exposed
• feeling inadequate—not having the answers
• saying the wrong thing and prompting a strong emotional response
• remembering and re-experiencing the pains of their own middle school years

Sometimes tweens fear
• being ridiculed or not taken seriously
• starting to express feelings and not being able to stop
• revealing their ignorance
• upsetting parents or having parents dwell on whatever the tween has mentioned
• triggering parental surveillance or punishment

Sometimes tweens and parents both fear:
• sitting in silence
• risking embarrassment
• being overwhelmed by the task
• having little in common
• talking about faith issues

Directed conversation seems to be one of the best ways to get communication started. Why does it work?

⭐ Especially when parents have had limited experience, given their own parents' discomfort with dialogue, this offers something, which is better than nothing.

⭐ Parents and kids are not alone but surrounded with others who are making their own stumbling attempts at dialogue.

⭐ Someone else is directing the process, which takes the pressure off of the parents. They just have to follow the directions.

⭐ Some folks tend to try a little harder when they're in public.

⭐ This setting has the feel of a practice session rather than a prime-time performance, also reducing the pressure placed on both parents and tweens.

To Parents: Care for the World Together

Nothing brings a family together like doing something that all family members find meaningful.

Your tween is going to be learning that all of God's creation is interconnected. Every choice we make, including the way we treat each other, has a direct bearing on the health of God's creation. Tweens don't take these kinds of things lightly. Now is the best time in their lives to get them involved, to have them begin stretching outside of themselves.

Tweens care about what happens in the world, and yet they have very short attention spans; there is so much competing for their time and attention (just like there is for all of us).

Parents want to have a good relationship with their tweens, just as their tweens are becoming independent and trying to pull away. However, doing something together that has real meaning can help keep a family relationship healthy and interesting to a preteen.

Every study shows that what preteens want is more of your time, so how about everyone in the family sitting down together, looking at their interests and talents, and coming up with a way to make God's world a better place. (It doesn't have to be a big and spectacular project; sometimes it's the little things that end up touching a soul, and the cumulative effect of small things really adds up.)

You must let your tweens have a real say in what you do as a family project. It is the only way they will feel that they really count. You must also hold them accountable for doing their part. It is the only way they will mature into responsible adults.

☞ Some possible things to do? ☜

✤ Adopt a single mother at the church. Take her an occasional meal. If she doesn't have family close by, invite her and her family over for Mother's Day, Easter, or some other celebration.

✤ Serve a meal to the homeless together.

✤ Grow vegetables and give the surplus to a food kitchen or put them out on a table at the church for those who need vegetables to pick up.

✤ Volunteer together to help on clean-up day at your local school, if your community has such an opportunity.

✤ Get together and send Grandmother and Grandfather an e-mail to which you have all contributed once every week.

Whatever choices you make, they must be yours.
Communication, understanding, and working as partners, as well as prayer, are key.

Faith Friends Program

A Faith Friend is an older person who mentors a tween in the faith and who can be called upon in times of a "faith emergency." Faith Friends can be developed and used in different ways.

☆ Formal Program

You might wish to have a formal mentoring program where you carefully pair up each tween with a specific Faith Friend and these Faith Friends could work actively as partners in the service/mission project you choose for these sessions.

☞ **Caution:** If this approach is used be sure that you have ways to ensure that the tweens get to do most of the talking and/or work.

If you use this as a formal mentoring program, have your Faith Friends call or e-mail your tweens at least once a week.

☆ Semi-Formal Program

You might wish to choose another group that meets at the same time and have them come to the first and last sessions of your "Making a World of Difference" sessions. Depending upon the numbers of tweens, Faith Friends might be assigned one or more tweens or tweens might be assigned one or more Faith Friends. (Young adult or older adult classes work best for mentoring this age group.)

Tweens choose from the available adults who will be the person they would call on if they have questions of faith or just want to talk about what's happened at school

☞ **Caution:** Educate your adult class beforehand. They must agree to be willing to talk with a tween if called or e-mailed.

☆ Informal Program

Let the tween choose somebody in the church that they feel comfortable with to be a person that he or she would choose to call or e-mail if they feel they need a Faith Friend to talk with.

• No matter which type of Faith Friend program you use, hand out a card to each tween and to each mentor and let them exchange phone numbers and e-mail addresses.

CAUTION: DO NOT ENCOURAGE TWEENS AND FAITH FRIENDS TO MEET ALONE AT ANY TIME.

• **IMPORTANT:** PARENTAL PERMISSION MUST BE OBTAINED FOR ANY INVOLVEMENT IN THE FAITH FRIENDS PROGRAM.

Affirmation of Us

I am a child of God.

I know God created me.

I am worthwhile.

I am valuable as I am.

Faith Friends Emergency Card

name

Faith Friend's name

Faith Friend's phone number

Faith Friend's e-mail address

Faith Friends Emergency Card

name

Faith Friend's name

Faith Friend's phone number

Faith Friend's e-mail address

Faith Friends Emergency Card

name

Faith Friend's name

Faith Friend's phone number

Faith Friend's e-mail address

Faith Friends Emergency Card

name

Faith Friend's name

Faith Friend's phone number

Faith Friend's e-mail address

Faith Friends Emergency Card

name

Faith Friend's name

Faith Friend's phone number

Faith Friend's e-mail address

Faith Friends Emergency Card

name

Faith Friend's name

Faith Friend's phone number

Faith Friend's e-mail address

Faith Friends Emergency Card

name

Faith Friend's name

Faith Friend's phone number

Faith Friend's e-mail address

Faith Friends Emergency Card

name

Faith Friend's name

Faith Friend's phone number